A Girl's Guide to Starting High School

using this book...

This book is designed to be interactive, and your silent friend! You might want to read this with a parent, guardian, someone you trust or keep it to yourself – it's up to you. There are parts of the book that you can write in and you can do this at your own pace.

It is designed to be your 'go to' guide in the preparation and first weeks of high school and it is also intended to be the book that you look back on in a few years' time and remind yourself of how you felt when you were entering into this new stage, and how far you have come as a young woman!

Over the next few years, you will change in body, mind and spirit (everyone does in their tween and teenage years). It's important to get to know yourself now, look after yourself now and into the future and when possible, surround yourself with people that are kind, fun, loving and caring towards you.

Yes, there will be some hiccups along the way; it won't always be easy. In fact, it will be really tricky sometimes. That's one of the reasons I have written this book. Don't worry – things that feel like a big deal at the time are often the things that will make you a stronger woman in the future.

That's a while away yet, so let's get started!

You have brains in your head,
You have feet in your shoes,
You can steer yourself in any direction you choose.
Dr Seuss

I wish you well, and trust this book will assist you in having a positive experience at the start of this new adventure in your school life.

Love, *Chloe*

Contents page

Welcome

Hello!

This is the start of an exciting new chapter of your life and as with anything new, it's filled with a lot of questions – the anticipation of entering into the unknown. This may be the first time you are venturing somewhere new and it will DEFINITELY not be the last!

If there is one thing that you need to remember as you make the transition into high school it's this – you are not the only one feeling the way you do right now! Every single Year 6 student is in the same situation. Some may have the advantage of having older siblings or cousins that have gone before them, but they haven't actually done it yet themselves.

Here's how other kids have felt towards the end of Year 6:

Grace – High school should be easy, I'm ready for this, let's just get there already – I am so over being at primary school – I want more independence and I want to wear a different uniform already!

Farah – I'm really nervous and excited right now – it changes on the day as to which one I am feeling. I'm talking about it all the time and I'd like someone to tell me that it's going to be okay.

Ruby – I feel a bit excited and nervous but I want to ease the nerves of a couple of my friends, they are feeling much more wound up about than me! I am thinking more about my friends than I am about myself right now.

Olivia – I don't want to talk to anyone about how I feel because I'm scared they will judge me. I'm just trying to put it to the back of my mind until it gets closer to the time. I want to know how I'm going to get to school, where the classrooms are and what the timetable is so I know what's going to happen.

But first... let's celebrate finishing primary school.

What three happy memories or achievements could you capture for when you look back at your primary school years?

1) _teachers_

2) _bees_

3) _writting_

What makes you proud of these memories or achievements?

1) ....

2) ....

3) ....

Helpful hint 1: Jog your memory back a few years if you can't think of anything more recent – it doesn't matter how long ago it was.

Helpful hint 2: It doesn't matter if it's a small, like going on camp without crying, or making a new friend, getting homework done when it's hard. Small things lead to bigger things down the way.

All the little things you do and the tiny steps you take often add up to the big things you remember.

When you haven't experienced something before, you may feel a few things, like...

- 💗 worried
- 💗 enthusiastic
- 💗 scared
- 💗 excited
- 💗 curious.

It's completely normal... it's called maturing, growing, changing. You haven't been here before so it is going to be a bit weird or uncomfortable. That's what will continually happen to varying degrees for the rest of your life! Imagine if you never changed – what would that be like?

A note to consider: Change is hard. It's hard for children and adults alike. It is a guarantee that you will learn as you go – you are not expected to know the answers yet and all of this is preparing you for the future.

Don't look back, you're not going that way.
Unknown

The story so far

In the last year of primary school, the teachers work with you to focus on what to expect for your first year of high school (and beyond). No matter how much it's talked about, it's sometimes quite difficult to picture.

You might have:

- friends outside of school through playing sport or having certain hobbies so you don't rely only on school friends;

- already changed schools before so you're comfortable meeting new people; or

- been at the same school with the same teachers for the whole of primary school, so you feel comfortable and you can't think of going anywhere else. Now people are talking bus timetables, class timetables, and a whole pile of different ways of working – it can all sound a bit overwhelming.

You may be going to high school with all of your primary school friends – that can be great because they are familiar but you may also be thinking: I can't wait to meet some new faces! Or maybe you're going to a school where you know no one – daunting and exciting all at the same time, or any combination of these. No matter what you are thinking, starting something new always takes a bit of courage.

Courage means you are scared but you ride the wave anyway!

Here are some reflections from current older students about their initial high school experience:

Jade – I was so sick of everyone at primary school. High school gave me so many more options for meeting new friends with different interests – it was so much better than what I expected it to be!

Mia – No one prepared me for the size of the playground at high school – there are so many people and they are all competing for the same small place to sit. At primary school we had a sports field to run around in.

Lilly – I wish I was more confident to ask questions in class – I do that now in Year 10 but I should have done it from the beginning!

Sophie – I had moved schools a few times because I was in foster care so I thought that would prepare me – what I didn't realise was that there were boys with full-on moustaches who towered above me and I felt like a dwarf – it was really intimidating but I got used to it after a few weeks!

Jasmine – I loved being able to start afresh – I created a new me – the me I wanted to be. I knew no one and I really did become the person I had always wanted to be in primary school – it's just great!

Hannah – I was surprised how many kids were on their phones at lunch – I found it boring so I asked a couple of new friends if they *wanted to play handball. I thought it was just a primary school thing, but heaps of people joined us!*

This is the start of your transition from being a BIG fish in a small tank to a SMALL fish in a big tank! It's the start of growth and change.

So where are we going to start?

Let's kick off by – looking after yourself!

For you to be in a 'get ready' mindset (ready to get started on this new stage of your schooling), you need a few ingredients:

- ♡ level of **self-awareness** so that you know what works for you and what doesn't

- ♡ **nutritious food** to give you energy and to make you feel good inside and out

- ♡ **exercise** to help you with focus, making friends and managing emotions

- 💟 **friends** and people around you to give you support and nurture you to be yourself

- 💟 **sleep** to give yourself the best chance at being in the right frame of mind for all things new

- 💟 **balanced screen time** to give you an outlet, connect with friends and know when to get off it!

- 💟 oh wait – and the **attitude** you know will serve you well for kick-off!

Pretty exhausting when you start to look at the list, so the next section is intended to make it as easy as possible for you to feel confident in your preparation.

Getting to know yourself

Your character

You are still going to be the same person when you get to high school but your environment will change significantly. With such a big change can come feelings of uncertainty and maybe nervousness. So it's important to be clear about who you are so you can navigate this new stage in your school years.

Yes, you know your name, your birthday and your favourite food. This section of your book is to help you learn about your character, your natural strengths and what is important to you – this will give you confidence and knowledge about why sometimes things feel great and why other times you can feel really uncomfortable.

Your character is who you are as a person – it's what's inside you, what makes you the girl you are. If someone were to say 'describe yourself', that can, for some, be a bit tricky. In understanding your own character, it can be easier to begin by thinking of someone you know really well or someone famous that inspires you. Describe them as if you are introducing them to someone else.

Try it out here:

Who are they?

....

What is it that you admire about them?

....

....

....

If you know them, how do they make you feel?

....

....

....

Whether you know them or not, how do you think they became who they are?

....

....

....

Now try this for yourself – how would you describe yourself? There is one rule: it is essential that the words are **descriptive** and **kind** – don't talk about who you are not, talk about who you are or who you would like to be in the future!

Write down a few words here (for example, funny, quirky, loud, quiet, patient, talkative, sensitive).

....

....

....

Molly – I tried to be someone I wasn't when I started high school. I'm glad that I don't do that anymore as it was really tiring and it didn't make me feel good – now I'm just me and my friends and I have fun and skateboard together. I don't have to think so much and I'm definitely not so worried about what others think about me!

Your strengths

Your strengths come naturally to you. It is much easier to work on what you are good at as opposed to what you are not good at. To find out what your strengths are, there is a free tool that you can access as long as your parent or guardian allows you to access this and they / you have an email address. The survey can be found at:

https://www.viacharacter.org/survey/account/register#youth

The survey will take about 15 minutes and will then give you a report listing your top character strengths. The report includes the definitions of the strength so it will help you understand what they mean. You can then use these as your superpowers in the future! You can print them out if you have a printer or copy them into this section. Knowing your strengths can help you with your friends, homework and hobbies. Sometimes though, and more importantly, they can help you when dealing with challenges or new situations, such as starting high school!

If you can't or don't want to access this really great tool, you can choose from some of the examples below. (The survey is definitely the better option!)

Loyalty 💗 Kindness 💗 Humour 💗 Spirituality
Love 💗 Leadership 💗 Forgiveness 💗 Teamwork
Honesty 💗 Bravery 💗 Gratitude 💗 Hope
Appreciation of Beauty 💗 Love of learning

Write them down here. For example: 'Kindness – this means doing favours and good deeds for others; helping them; taking care of them.' (Source VIA Character Strengths)

.... this means ....

.... this means ....

.... this means ....

.... this means ....

.... this means ....

What do you feel when you look at your strengths? Write a few words or a few sentences. For example: I feel more confident or I feel proud or I understand why I am the way I am.

....

....

....

When do you think you can use these strengths? For example: organising your homework, playing sport, going to a party, going to the shops to buy groceries...

....

....

....

Your values

What's important to you is probably different to what is important to others. That's what makes us all unique.

Another way of getting to know yourself and understanding how you see the world, how you make decisions and how you understand people in general is through your values. Your values are like a shining star up in the sky that help guide you. Imagine you are out at sea in a boat, all by yourself, and you are told to look at the brightest star to guide you home. Well, your values are that star!

Note: There are no right or wrong values, they just make up part of who you are as a powerful, knowledgeable girl.

So, what's important to you?

Here are some examples below. You can circle a maximum of six or create your own list:

🤍 academic success   🤍 being popular

🤍 being clean and organised   🤍 being kind

- being curious
- loving learning
- family
- laughing every day
- having money
- having lots of clothes and jewellery
- playing sport

- being creative
- being able to forgive others
- helping others
- health
- my religion
- being persistent (continuing to try when it feels really tough!)

Write down each of the values here and what makes them very important to you:

1) ....

....

2) ....

....

3) ....

....

4) ....

....

5) ....

....

6) ....

....

You can also write them down on a piece of paper and decorate it if you like. You could make a few copies and stick them in a few different places like your pencil case, your diary, your sock drawer, your phone. You can always refer to them when you are in a tough situation or faced with a difficult decision. They will help be your guide!

You have an amazing power – no one else is YOU! How exciting to get to know yourself better...

A secret tip: when you act in line with your values it will make you feel happier and more confident in yourself because it feels right!

It's also important to remember that during your tween and teenage years, what's important may change but if you know them now, then you can update and adjust along the way.

An example of values in action:

Georgie – I tried really hard at school but I didn't seem to get the results I wanted. I thought one of my values was academic results but then I realised that it was persistence – never giving up! Now I find it easier to keep going when its hard and apply this in other ways with sport and with my friends when things are a bit tough going.

Don't be confused between what people say you are and who you know you are.
Oprah Winfrey

Different kinds of smarts!

Okay, so, a few words of advice around school and education. It is not supposed to be easy!

Learning is lifelong so you are not expected to finish Year 6 knowing more than you already do and you are not expected to leave school in Year 12 and know everything about the rest of your life.

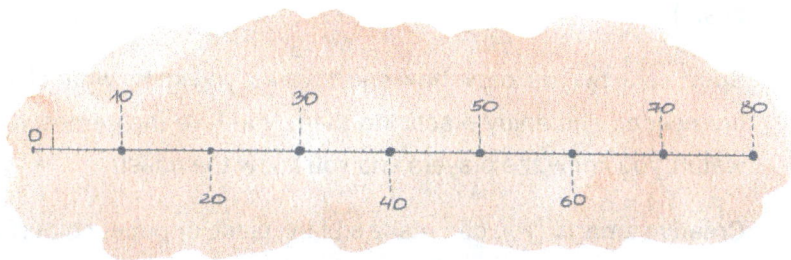

Mark your age here – look how far you have to go in your life-long journey – don't rush and don't stress.

A lot of people don't find school easy because it's a lot more than just rocking up to class each day to learn the academics. There will be some people you come across in life that won't be your kind of people. School is for you to start to learn how to get along with others that you wouldn't normally choose to be with. There is more about that in the section *Exploring tricky situations* but for now we can look at the fact that there are different kind of smarts and it is important to recognise what yours are.... this helps you to build your confidence when you know what your natural 'smart is'.

Some examples:

- 💜 **Academic smarts** (learning comes easily to you and you get high marks without too much thought.)

- 💜 **People smarts** (you understand how to get the best out of people, you are empathetic and you know what makes people tick.)

💗 **Emotional smarts** (being aware of how you feel, why you feel the way you do, then knowing how to deal with the feelings you have so that you can look after yourself in different situations.)

💗 **Street smarts** (you know how to get about, you can work out tricky situations, you are a survivor.)

💗 **Money smarts** (you know the value of money; you know what's a good way to spend your money and you know how to save your cash.)

💗 **Sport smarts** (you know how sport works; you know what skills are needed and enjoy practising them, you love the games you watch, you know the players and you know the rules!)

💗 **Creative smarts** (you can make a blank piece of paper colourful and beautiful in no time, you can visualise or decorate a room with flair, you experiment with food by cooking up a storm in the kitchen or you just love creating anything you think is beautiful.)

💗 **Nature smarts** (you know the names of the trees, flowers, animals and all things nature. You do your best to care for the environment.)

Write down any other kinds of smart:

....

....

Detail here what you believe your 'smart' strength is:

....

....

Where can you use this?

....

....

Have you used this as much as you can?   Yes / No

If you would like to increase your smarts, what area would it be in?

....

....

How do you think you could do this?

....

....

Looking after yourself

The way you talk to yourself matters!

To feel good, it is important to treat yourself respectfully – what you say to yourself impacts how you feel and how you speak to and treat others. For some of you, this section is a brief introduction on how to start to be aware of your inner voice. For those of you who have been introduced to this before, it might be a helpful reminder. Below are some powerful words to remember:

Let your inner voice be the kindest voice you hear.
Anonymous

Without thinking about it, we talk negatively and positively to ourselves, sending messages to our brain that can then impact the way we feel. To have a healthy mind and outlook it is helpful to be aware of your balance of positive and negative thoughts. If there are more positive than negative thoughts – that is healthy, if there are more negative than positive, you could be being very hard on yourself.

Helpful hint: Try treating yourself like your own best friend. Sound a bit strange? Well for those of you who have a great friend, the likelihood is that you are kind, caring, supportive and loyal to them. Imagine how you would feel if you treated yourself this way!

Looking after yourself and your thoughts will help you with believing in yourself, being kind to yourself, and being a great friend to others. For many of us, we are nicer to other people than we are to ourselves and if this is applicable to you, it is important that this stops NOW! It isn't helpful and it doesn't make us kinder people. We are often tough markers and can make a judgement about ourselves quickly.

Here are a couple of helpful hints to keep your inner voice on track:

- If a negative thought comes into your head – ask yourself, is this thought helpful?

  Most of the time it will be 'NO' – see if you can 'flip' the thought. Think about the opposite or at least a more positive way of talking to yourself. If you think – I'm going to fail this maths test, try to flip it to – Just because maths is challenging for me, doesn't mean I can't pass this test with a bit of extra study or asking for help from the teacher.

- When there is something you find tough to deal with, think about what you know you CAN do about it, not what you CAN'T do about it. For example, if you have a friend who is unkind to you, you can't control what they say or do but you CAN control what you say and do in response.

I'm ok with having bad dance moves. I'm ok with having horrible lower teeth, that's what makes me me and for some reason that's worked out alright.

Katy Perry

If you start talking negatively to yourself, the great thing is that you have noticed it – that's an important first step, now you can do something about it.

Ask yourself: would I say this to someone else?

If you answered no, because you wouldn't want to hurt that person's feelings, then STOP. What can you say to yourself that is more kind?

For example: If you catch yourself saying, "I'm not good enough to make the netball or soccer team", try saying, "I will give it a go, I have been improving and getting better over the last couple of seasons so I will give trying out a go." Another one is "I'm not good at science." Try saying, "Science is harder for me than other subjects, so I know I need to work harder to understand and learn, I haven't got it yet and I will get there."

When you are doing it tough:

- give yourself the right ingredients, what makes YOU feel better? Is it playing with your pet? Cooking and sharing some biscuits? Reading a book or chatting to a friend?

- do a random act of kindness – surprise someone by doing something kind for them and it will probably make you feel better, too!

- if you feel you are doing it more tough than the other kids around you, then please speak to a counsellor, a parent, a guardian or someone you can trust – we all need a helping hand sometimes and it's okay to ask for help.

Ava – I go for a run at the park when I feel unhappy or sad – it just helps me zone out. Once I get home I feel more relaxed and more myself again.

Be strong enough to stand alone, smart enough to know when you need help, and brave enough to ask for it.
Ziad Abdelnour (Author)

When someone else is doing it tough:

- 💗 look out for opportunities to be kind – a little kindness goes a long way.

- 💗 could you help a friend with some suggestions for what works for you and give them some options?

- 💗 talk to an adult that you trust.

Building your energy levels

A bit about moving your body....

When you were little, you ran around because it was fun and you didn't even think about it. As you get older, many girls can become increasingly less active or for some of us a bit lazy – you might enjoy more screen time and sit around chatting more often. When you get to high school there is generally less physical activity in the timetable, and this can make you feel less likely to do more activity!

FACT: When you do less your brain gets used to this and so does your body and before you know it, everything can become a bit of a challenge! Perhaps some of you will not want to do exercise at all.

FACT: Exercise gives you energy, it doesn't zap your energy.

Isla – I have done less exercise at high school because there isn't the same playground set up – I don't run around at lunchtime and recess like I used to and I wondered why I was starting to feel a bit down.

19

If you don't feel like exercising, remind yourself of four things:

1) **Your body is built to move** – choose a physical activity that you have either enjoyed in the past or one that you are curious about – ask a friend or family member to join you or do it by yourself. You could go to the park for a walk or run, walk on the beach, participate in a team sport, use a skipping rope or shoot hoops. Walking to the bus stop or train station to get some extra steps in also counts! One way of positively using your phone could be to do a workout on YouTube – it's free and you can do it any time. Look up yoga, dance workouts and skills training for any movement you are interested in.

2) **Something is better than nothing** – if you are someone who isn't active, start with five minutes a day in the first week and build yourself up over the first term to an hour a day EVERY day! Before you know it, you won't even think about it. It will become part of your daily way of doing things.

If you don't manage it every day – don't be down on yourself – aim for the next day and plan to make it work in with what you have got on.

3) **Make it easy for yourself** – a couple of suggestions: when you wake up in the morning and if you have time, get straight into your sports stuff and runners and get on with it OR do it at a time of the day or week that you know is a natural time to do it – mornings work for loads of people because it gets it out of the way! Another way of doing it is when you get back from school, put your runners on and go for a walk or do half your homework and then go and do your exercise of choice.

4) **Reward yourself** – what do you love that you could reward yourself with? Make sure you note down what you have done and that will help remind you of what works! You could try:

- getting out in nature

- laughing – watch a funny movie, pull a fun prank on a parent or guardian, make a ridiculous face in the mirror or remember a funny story from when you were younger!

- listening or dancing to music – put on uplifting, feel-good music, the type of music you listen to affects how you feel so if you want to be energised, listen to energising music

- singing – in the shower or in your room if you feel a bit self-conscious!

- fresh air – even when you are in the car, put the window down and feel the air in your face and hair – it will make you feel alive!

- sunlight (always in moderation)

- decluttering your room – yes, maybe a last option for some but it makes you feel better when you are in a pleasant environment. Even making your bed or having a decluttered space will help you feel like you have it together!

Your food

When you get to high school, they don't do breaks for fresh fruit and vegetables so you are on your own with what you eat and when – how liberating!

Some parents and guardians give more freedom to their kids when it comes to deciding what's in the lunchbox and some kids ask for more responsibility now that they are moving to a more independent environment.

If your parent/guardian hasn't given you this responsibility yet, suggest to them that you could do it as a trial for a couple of weeks. Then they can give you feedback on what they have witnessed before committing to this new routine.

This sort of responsibility comes from building trust with your parent/guardian. The more independence you expect, the more responsibility your parent/guardian will expect from you. Here are some suggestions to show them you can make sensible choices:

1) Propose a budget for how much your family can spend on lunches for the week and stick to that budget. Budgeting will serve you well for the rest of your life so why not start now! You could already be helping by doing the weekly shop in your house, but if you aren't, this is another great way of contributing and learning about what options are out there. You may realise that the reason you have certain foods as a treat is because they are more expensive!

2) Make choices that you know are good for your body. It can be easy to think that breakfast isn't important or to start missing meals when you are busy or because you think you don't need extra food as your body changes. It is really important you know what's right so make sure you

fuel yourself for the day ahead and that it's balanced – have the chips and chocolate biscuit if you want and make sure that you have the fruit and veggies, too.

3) Handy hint – eat foods the way they were grown (have an apple instead of dried apples in a packet; have grapes instead of a roll-up; have dried cereal instead of a muesli bar; have an apricot instead of apricot bites; have a banana instead of a banana muffin... you get the drift).

4) Are you bored of sandwiches yet? Having a sandwich 5 times a week for 40 weeks is 200 sandwiches per year – so if you have eaten a sandwich every school day since the start of school then you have already had a minimum of 1,400 sandwiches, and by the end of high school this number will be 2,800! The great thing about sandwiches is that they're easy – most people have bread in their cupboard. Maybe consider mixing it up? If your budget allows, go for a wrap instead or pre-cooked rice and salad, a cold toastie (yes, it's still a sandwich but it has a different consistency), crackers and cheese, rice crackers and a dip? You can even bring leftovers from the night before. Check out this website for some handy hints:

https://heas.health.vic.gov.au

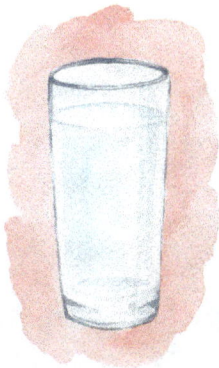

5) Have something for FREE – water! It's the only drink you need – all the others are non-essential and most of the time they're not good for you.

Remember – what you put into your body contributes to how you feel, so look at eating as an opportunity to look after your body and fuel it for energy and growth. Be kind to your body and give it the nutrients and water that it needs to grow and give you energy that lasts throughout the day. These choices will contribute to your overall wellbeing.

A note on your body:

It's important to listen to what your body is telling you. This can be a bit tricky since it may be changing a lot at the moment. Perhaps by now you are wearing a crop top and have your period. If you haven't yet, remember that we all develop at different rates and when you are having your period, you will feel different to your 'normal'. If you do have your period, you may find it easier to manage at high school than primary school. For example, the toilets will be set up better. Be kind to yourself, look after yourself and tell a parent or guardian so they know what's going on for you. This is also when the fruit, veggies and general good diet are really important.

Since I don't look like every other girl, it takes a while to be ok with that. To be different. But different is good.
Serena Williams
(Professional tennis player and fashion designer)

Phones / Social media

Some of you may have had a phone during primary school. For others, you have had to wait until you get to high school (or later). There are many reasons for this – your parents or guardian, no matter what you think, have made the decision with your best interests at heart.

If you are new to the phone world (or you are well into it!) here are a few tips and tricks:

- Your safety is the most important thing – if you feel uncomfortable or unsafe at any time, turn it off and tell an adult. Yes, it is that easy – your parent or guardian can help you navigate some of what is going on for you.

- When sending any message, send it as if you are talking to the person face-to-face.

- If you wouldn't say it to the person's face, don't type or emoji it.

- If you don't want to turn it off and you know what you have been sent isn't appropriate you can take a screenshot. Be aware that some apps notify others when screenshots are taken. Ask someone you trust to take a photo of the content of the screen and get another person's opinion if you think that will help you decide on what's appropriate and what's not.

- If you wouldn't put the picture on your wall, don't post it.

- It is still important to speak and see people face-to-face – we need this for our overall connection and wellbeing.

💗 It is important to make sure you have other things going on in your life other than what happens through the screen. This can be hard when there is a pandemic, so have a think about whether you have other interests. If you don't, then you could consider trying something new like a sport, music, a craft, a hobby or even walking your neighbour's dog if you don't have one yourself.

💗 Social media accounts require you to be 13 so don't break the law this early in your life – it's not a great start.

💗 Phone apps are made so that you want to go on them all the time! They are designed to be addictive and it's really important to have a level of self-discipline if your parent or guardian trusts you with your phone 24 hours a day. What do you think is a reasonable amount of time to be staring at a small screen? (Be honest with yourself!) It might help to think about how this time balances with other stuff you have going on and see where you are spending most of your time. For example, if you are on it four hours a night and you don't speak to anyone else or do any exercise that isn't a good balance for your wellbeing. Try and reduce the screen time and increase in another area.

💗 People aren't always who they say they are. Make sure your privacy settings are on your phone and that everyone you are connected with is who you have met in person.

💗 Dim the screen to avoid straining your eyes.

You are not supposed to know what to do in all situations so reach out and seek help – it's a really great lesson in life to ask for help. The more you ask, the easier it should become and it might be different people depending on the situation.

Sleep matters!

No matter how many hours you 'think' you need, it is a FACT that a girl between 10 and 13 needs 9–11 hours sleep. You can go onto sleepeducation.org to get access to a sleep calculator.

So what happens if you don't get enough sleep?

You might: get upset over small things, get angry, find learning or focusing more challenging, feel sad for no real reason, have a tired feeling all the time and maybe even be a bit snippy!

You might end up eating more. When your body is tired, your brain says, 'do something to make me feel better' and depending on your way of thinking, that can be to eat more food. Eating more food and doing less exercise because you feel tired can mean that you start to feel uncomfortable. This cycle then turns into a habit and will only make you feel worse.

Nadia – When I'm tired, I get grumpy at my parents. I pretend to my friends that I am fine @ school but when I get home from school, I just let loose at whoever is around. My family know it's not how I normally am so they try to just stay away!

Amalie – I forget things more easily and I can't find where I put my stuff when I don't sleep properly!

Claire – I can't focus on school or sport and feel like I'm in a separate bubble to everyone else – it's pretty weird!

If you think you could do with some extra sleep, tick the box for what you could try:

- ☐ Don't have your phone in the bedroom or in bed

- ☐ If you use your phone for an alarm to wake you up in the morning, put it on flight mode – this way the alarm will still work but your notifications will be off

- ☐ Don't go on your phone an hour before bed

- ☐ Listen to quiet music instead of playing games that involve focus and excitement

- ☐ Read a book to help relax your brain

- ☐ Practise slow and long breaths to relax your body (see p 43 for how to do this)

- ☐ Write in a journal about what you are grateful for – best way to finish the day! (More on journaling later.)

- ☐ Get ear plugs if you share a room with someone else

- ☐ Put socks on for bed – it can help you get to sleep!

Sleepovers

Sleepovers are nothing new for many of you. If you had sleepovers at friends' houses in primary school, your parents or guardian would generally know the parents of your friend. With new friends it's a bit trickier since they are unfamiliar to your parents, so if you are going to a new friend's house for a sleepover or even just to hang out, don't be surprised if your parent or guardian is asking a few more questions or even saying that they want to talk to the other parent before you go – they are looking out for you.

Sleepovers can be great fun! If you are the type of girl who can stay up until 3am and still feel great the next day then you are a real winner! Not everyone can have that abundance of energy so if you know that you operate with more sleep, it may be best to arrange to catch up with your new friends in a different way – during the day. Yes, you might get a bit of FOMO but if you can be honest with your friends and say, 'Every so often I can have a sleepover but I can't do it every weekend', your good friends will respect you and even laugh with you about it.

It's good to talk....

Some of us come from families where we are encouraged to talk about our feelings. Others of us come from families where we don't talk about the way we feel because it's just not the way we approach our life.

When you are going through a big change it can really help to have a couple of people you know you can reach out to at any time, someone you can trust. They might be a friend, a teacher, a parent or another family member. For some of you, it may even be your pet – to talk out loud about how you are feeling can sometimes be exactly what you need!

Often you will find that when you open up about how you feel, the person you are sharing your feelings with will share theirs too and then you will realise:

1) you are not alone

2) people generally really enjoy solving problems and many people find that it makes them feel good to help someone out or offer their advice.

3) There is an old saying, 'a problem shared is a problem halved' (Katie John). It basically means that when you share what's going on, the problem can be made easier. After all, two minds are better than one. The person you are speaking to might have experienced a similar issue in the past and by working together you can find a solution.

Caution: choose your audience wisely, especially if they are a new friend. When you have new friends, it can sometimes take a while for you to feel comfortable being yourself. There are some girls that don't have the maturity to keep someone else's story to themselves and they can use it against you – it's a really tricky balance and it's a lifelong lesson that you continue to encounter. In some situations, unless you say 'please keep this to yourself' or 'please don't tell anyone' then it can be seen as an easy story to pass on to someone else, and even making these requests won't make a difference. Keep this in mind when sharing.

A note on 'secrets': If you are the person receiving messages like 'please don't tell anyone else' and 'do you promise not to tell anyone else?' you should understand that it is really important to respect that message. There is one EXCEPTION (and that's a massive **exception**) – when you are worried for the safety and wellbeing of the other person, or yourself if you feel uncomfortable. If you feel they are in a dangerous or upsetting situation or what they tell you makes you uncomfortable, then it is **essential** to tell an adult who you trust about what you have been told. The adult can then decide what to do with the information.

Listen to what your body is telling you. Your body is generally right. The sensations in your tummy – which could be butterflies or a churning feeling – might mean that something doesn't sit right with you. Then you need to decide what to do about it. To help you with this you can speak to a friend, a relative or a teacher.

So what happens if you don't like to talk?

You can write down your thoughts and keep them to yourself. It can make you feel better when you write your feelings down – and this includes all feelings – the good, the bad, the confusing, the overwhelming and the celebrations!

Some people keep diaries or journals. A journal entry might look like this (and this is an opportunity to try it out):

Today was

....

A standout for me today was

....

I felt

....

I didn't like

....

I wish

....

I am grateful for

....

I'm looking forward to

....

When we start to capture what is going on for us it can be really helpful for our overall wellbeing. Of particular importance is a note on finding things to be grateful for.

It can be basic stuff like what you had for breakfast, the weather, kind words from someone. As long as you can press 'pause' from everything going on and capture what you may sometimes take for granted.

Angie writes daily in a diary or journal about how she is feeling. This helps 'get it out'. Angie also started writing down one good thing that happened during the day. After a few weeks Angie said, 'I felt more positive by getting all my thoughts on the page and then making sure I acknowledged one thing in the day that I am grateful for.'

If you don't want to talk and you don't want to write, that's okay too – these are just a couple of options to consider so you don't feel like you are doing it all alone.

Study and exams

It's a real shift for most of you when you head to high school – you go from a bit of homework (for some primary schools there is no compulsory homework) to multiple deadlines from different teachers, essays, exams for key subjects and a multitude of different classes, subjects and places to be!

It takes a bit of getting used to and it won't take long to adjust – it's the same old story – when you do something new it takes more energy and focus which can be a challenge and you need to be in the right mindset to adapt. Before you know it, you will be more confident in how you approach your preparation and organisation.

To help start you off it's good to know that different people have different learning styles.

At high school you will most likely use your laptop for all of your work in class and for the submission of assessments. To help you take notes, absorb information and keep it in your brain, it is important to know the easiest way you learn.

There is a survey you can download to help with this on https://kids.lovetoknow.com.

Now that you know how to make it easier for yourself in learning what you are taught and preparing for homework, what do you need to do?

....

....

Understanding how you learn can help you have a positive approach to school. The power of positive thinking helps with a growth mindset... that's what we are going to cover next! Having a growth mindset is essential for your journey through high school (and life!).

Growth mindset – giving things a red hot go, knowing that it's tough and that you aren't always going to get it right. Think about practising and always improving – you're not going to be a beginner at science or maths forever. Learning is life-long – learning is not just school based and when you realise that, your brain will continue to learn and 'grow' in the future.

Top tips for study and homework

1) Spend 10 minutes each school night going over what you learned that day – schedule this time before dinner or after dinner so that you don't forget to do it.

2) DON'T leave it until the last minute – this will set you and maybe your family into a level of distress really quickly. Write down or put in your phone the due date and make it visible so you don't forget!

3) Don't be surprised if you are used to getting top marks and all of a sudden you are scoring average marks. High school expectations regarding quality of work are much higher and it will take time to adjust to the new expectations. Putting on your 'growth hat' will allow you to be curious about what it is you need to do both MORE of and LESS of to keep getting better marks that represent your confidence in the subject you are studying.

4) Remind yourself that the exams are also a measure for the teacher on how well they are teaching you.

5) For the majority of us, we need to continuously and consistently chip away at the process of learning – nothing easy will come overnight. This means that you have to find a way to include study as part of your

day-to-day routine. If you are an early riser – make it easy and do some learning over breakfast or if you are a night owl do it at night – know what works for you and time it well.

6) Most schools will provide you with marking or marking rubric criteria for the assessments and tasks you need to submit. Look at these criteria – make it easier for yourself and the teacher marking it by responding to the assessment and completing everything they ask for. That way it becomes a checklist for you as you work through it – over time, this will become easier and you should get better results.

> Kat – I got a mini whiteboard that I put a study timetable on which made it visual for me to follow and it made me feel more mature in my approach to school. Colour coding different subjects was a really helpful approach.

If you are someone who gets really worried about all of this – here are a few words from Mia:

> Mia – I wish someone had told me that homework and assessments are not as big a deal as what I thought they were – I got really stressed, upset and angry and got to the point where I couldn't focus because I was so worried. If you try your hardest and you don't get a good mark, don't worry, you can still get into Year 8!

> Mistakes are proof that you are trying.
> Anonymous

Building your confidence

Confidence is like a muscle

Yes – the more you work at it, the stronger it will become.

Confidence is allowing yourself to try new things, understanding that it's not always going to be an amazing experience or outcome but giving things a go anyway.

If you feel worried about starting high school, it's normal. Most people feel worried when change happens. To help ease the worry and feel confident, it can help to focus on what you can do about this change and what you can't do about any situation you are faced with. Steven Covey, in his book *The seven habits of highly effective people*, uses the idea of three circles. You can draw these three circles for yourself either physically or in your mind (see next page):

In the centre you can ask yourself or write in what you can control about the situation you are in.

In the middle circle you write down what you can contribute or influence in the situation.

In the outside circle you write down what you have no control or influence over and what you have to 'let go'. Yep, just like that song that you heard over and over when you were little – 'let it go, let it go!'

Here are some examples of what you can control: your words to yourself and others, your actions, how much time you spend on your phone or tech, your reactions when you don't agree with someone, your attitude,

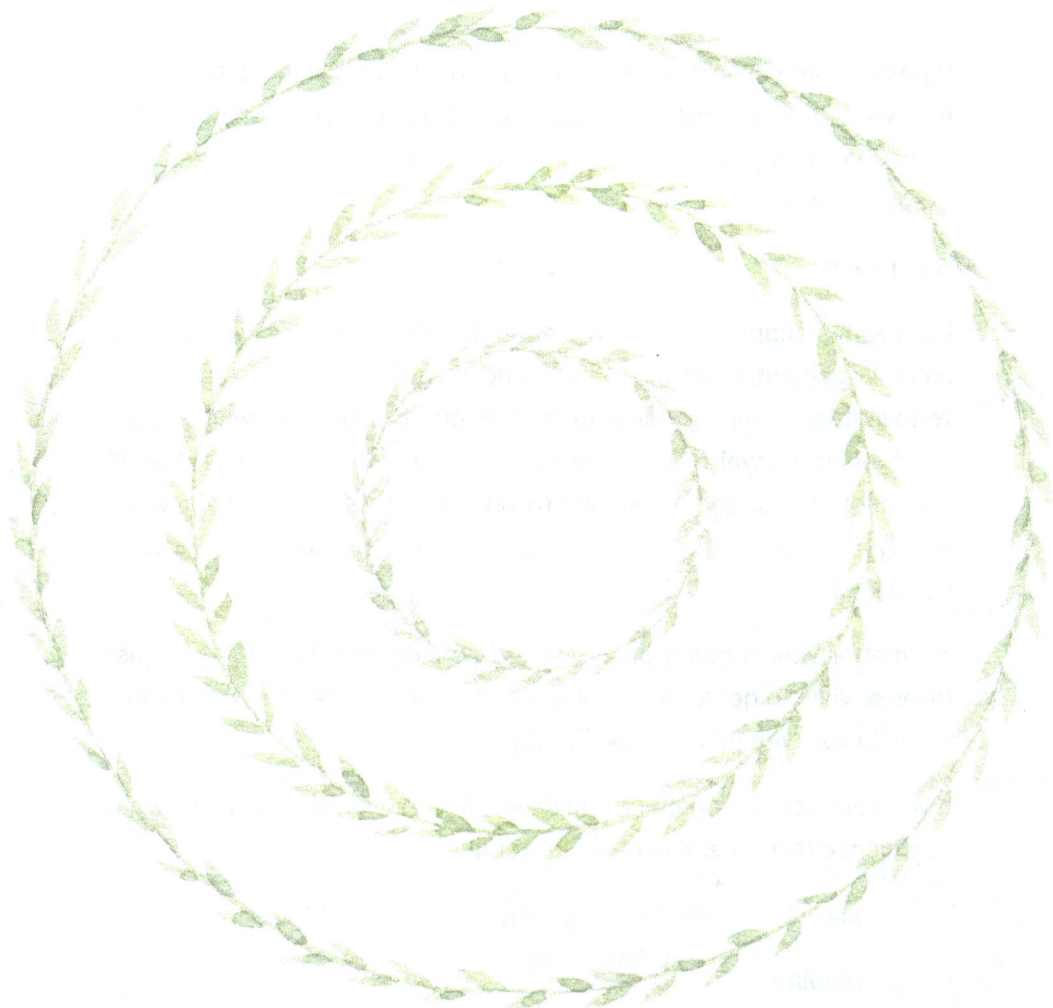

your values, asking for help, the friends you hang out with, how you react to your siblings and friends if they are annoying, doing good deeds and moving your body.

Here are some examples of what you can influence: your choices in food (because you are still a child who doesn't have complete control of the family budget when it comes to the grocery shop!), recycling in your home, your friends' feelings (yes, if your friend is in a bad mood you might be able to influence it and equally you might not), how much time you spend on homework as there may be competing priorities.

Here are some examples of what you should let go and maybe accept that you can't do anything about: your teachers, your siblings, your timetable, other people's behaviour, other people's actions, the weather, exams, pandemics / COVID.

Helpful hint: Give energy to what you can control!

In an earlier chapter we explored strengths. Strengths are what you are naturally good at, so it's likely that if one of your strengths is 'teamwork', you will feel confident doing team projects at school, playing a team sport, being a loyal friend or helping out someone in need. It doesn't take a lot of your energy. Similar to kindness, if it's a natural character strength of yours then you don't have to 'think' or build confidence in being kind.

No matter what's going on – you are confident at something. It just takes a while to get there! Look back at what you are 'smart' at as this will help you with thinking confidently.

If you think about something you do easily – that's when you know what confidence feels like. You may feel confident:

- playing a sport or playing a musical instrument

- reading

- knowing how to get the bus or train anywhere you need to be

- speaking to new people

- baking or cooking

- arts and crafts.

Nailing confidence is having the mindset to give it a go. You never know, you might just surprise yourself at how capable you are. Continuing to challenge yourself in this way will build what can be described as the confidence muscle in your brain.

Look at tying shoelaces – you had to practise and probably get someone else's help at first; most people don't do it easily the first few times. Now you don't even have to think twice – you are confident at tying your shoe-laces because it's easy for you, having practised the skill time and time again!

Acknowledging that we are all confident in some area of our lives is important.

Write down two situations when you feel confident:

1) ....

....

2) ....

....

How does it feel?

....

....

Write down two situations you would like to become more confident:

1) ....

....

2) ....

....

What would it feel like if you were to get more confidence?

....

....

Reflecting on the answers to these questions and then thinking about how you can apply them to a situation where you don't feel as confident should, in fact, help you develop confidence.

Ask yourself what you need for yourself to feel as confident as possible in your high school journey:

....

....

....

....

Top four tips for continuing to build your confidence muscle:

- 💜 speak kindly to yourself.

- 💜 be okay with not getting it the first time and remind yourself that you are 'giving it a go' – this builds the confidence muscle by trying and being okay with not nailing it each time.

- 💜 practise breathing – you can practise calm breathing by looking in the mirror, putting your hands around your ribs, take in a breath for four seconds, hold for four seconds and blow out for six seconds, making sure your mouth is closed and you are breathing through your nose. It can help keep you peaceful, calm and you should feel more relaxed. You can do this on your walk to school, in the playground, preparing for an assessment or going to sleep. Repeat this every time you want to feel more confident and calm in a situation. It will take practice and after practising you will become more confident in this way of breathing.

In:	1	2	3	4		
Hold:	1	2	3	4		
Out:	1	2	3	4	5	6

- 💜 the way you carry yourself – your body language tells your brain and other people how you are feeling a lot of the time. Your body language is more powerful than your words. If you hold your head high, your back straight and look people in the eye when you are talking to them, they are more likely to listen and you are more likely to feel good. Another way of describing this is having the wonder woman pose. If you are ever feeling 'unconfident', social psychologist Amy Cuddy has some advice around this – you look in the mirror with your back straight and you put your hands on your hips, ready for anything! If you are someone who hasn't thought about this before, maybe give it a go and see what a difference this can make.

A final note on confidence: It comes and goes. Sometimes you feel like you are doing amazingly, patting yourself on the back and thinking – I'm nailing this. Then the next time you do the same thing it doesn't work out. This is normal. Be patient and kind to yourself.

Becoming More Mature

The art of getting ready for high school is the expectation that you will be more mature in your approach to most things that are happening in your life.

Being more mature involves being able to understand and feel what others are experiencing – this is called empathy. Learning empathy is easy for some and harder for others. It involves understanding and being curious about what is going on for others in a supportive, caring and intentionally kind way.

Learning to stand in somebody else's shoes, to see through their eyes. Empathy is a quality of character that can change the world.
Barack Obama (former President of the USA)

This quote is not about being nosey or feeling that if someone is crying, you should cry too. Or when someone is angry, you are also angry.

Empathy is: being aware. Being there for someone and working out how you can help them voice how they feel, always remembering that you can't solve everyone's problems. It's listening.

Empathy is not: agreeing or doing something that someone else wants you to do, because of their situation.

Empathy is a skill you can learn. If it doesn't come naturally to you, think about when you have felt sad or disappointed.

What has someone else done for you, so that you know that they are with you and understand what's going on for you?

Situation:

....

....

Who was the person?

....

....

What did they do to make you feel like they understood and helped you?

....

....

Now think about what you could do to help others when using your empathy skills:

....

....

There are different types of personalities in this world and not everyone is like you – in fact, no one is exactly like you. What you may have realised is that sometimes you really like hanging out with similar types of friends and then other times you seem to get along with completely different or opposite personalities.

In six years' time, high school will be over – how would you like to look back on it? Friendships are important and as you know from primary school, they can make the difference in the level of enjoyment and fun you have over the next few years. You may keep your friends from primary school or you may make new friends along the way – try and keep yourself open to new friendships – you never know where they may lead. It's also really normal to move friendship groups as you change and grow. It's also normal for your friends to change their groups, too.

You may have picked up from this that there is no right or wrong!

To help you think about what type of friend you want to be, here is an opportunity for reflection and planning.

Do you have someone that makes you think – I would love to be like him or her when I 'grow' up?

....

Think about why that is.

Is it their stories? The way they make you feel? How they treat others? What they believe in? Jot down here who it is and why you think they are someone you would like to grow into for the future:

....

....

....

....

If you think about why you like your friends, it is generally because of the way they make you feel when you are hanging out. If you feel comfortable, confident and calm around them, then generally speaking, it means that they are the sort of person you want to hang out with. When you are being yourself it shouldn't require too much energy to be with them.

It is important to remember that it might take a bit of energy to meet your friends to begin with. Be active in finding your friends – it takes time and it takes your focus to give it a red hot go. Having one or two friends to start with is enough – as long as you know that they are your kinda girl (or boy). Remember to keep in touch with your friends from primary school too, if it feels right.

> Aisha – I love my friends because we have fun, we can be silly with each other and I know that if I tell them something that is serious they will listen.

This can take some time to get there, so make sure you are patient with yourself and your new friends while you are on this journey to find a new tribe or friendship group.

It's completely normal to feel awkward when you meet someone for the first time, but if this uncomfortable feeling continues over the next few months then maybe you need to consider if they are the right friend for you.

Introducing four different types of friends:

Emily is direct. She arrives at school ready for action, is quick to get on with her homework and is often focused on what's coming up next. Emily's competitive and confident, and generally says what she thinks.

A word of advice to Emily – your focus can sometimes be interpreted as disinterest. When your friends realise you are coming from a loving place, they will accept your directness more easily. Remember – some girls are more sensitive than you so make sure that when you have finished speaking, you check they are okay and have not misinterpreted your tone or body language.

Charlie is a social butterfly. She loves hanging out with her friends all the time! Charlie has a tendency to talk through class and is the one who organises all the after-school activities and sleepovers – she always has a friend over.

A word of advice to Charlie – remember that all of your friends have different personalities so they may need some time out from seeing you all the time. Although some will need space to recharge, they still love you and they will call you when they are ready to hang out!

Milla is a good listener. She is the type of friend that you can rely on for support and advice when you have a falling-out or misunderstanding with another friend. Someone like Milla will be the most supportive of the group and will try and make everything better when things go sour. She helps everyone move on and be friends again. Milla makes others feel calm around her while also having fun doing what you are all doing.

A word of advice to Milla – It is okay not to like everyone and in turn, not everyone will like you. It is better to keep true to yourself and allow others to be drawn to your kind heart, but be careful not to allow others to take advantage of you. If you spend too much energy on others, you might not have enough for yourself so if you start feeling a bit exhausted give yourself a break!

Saanvi is shy and reserved. She is the friend who is quieter or softly spoken who can come across as shy and may take a while to get her friend group together. She is diligent, generally very neat and tidy and likes to make sure that every decision she makes is the right one. If you are going to the shops with Saanvi, she will be the one you can rely on to find the best places to go and still get you home on time.

A word of advice to Saanvi – not everyone is as organised and focused as you. Your friends are loyal to you because you are you, yet you are the glue that holds everyone together. Sometimes they may not understand the way you prioritise things, so be patient with them when they are running late, talking too much or not thinking about things as deeply as you might otherwise.

So what should you do if you have a falling out or disagreement?

Being true to yourself and looking after your mental health is way more important than any friendship or relationship. Think what advice you would give to a friend in this situation and follow your own advice.

Telling others how you feel is important. Fall-outs and misunderstandings happen because a lot of the time we don't want to hurt the other person's feelings.

Consider speaking your mind if you feel in your gut it's the right thing to do. Do it because you care about the other person, not because you have any intention of making them feel bad about themselves. Your voice might shake and it might be a bit clunky but each time you do this you will feel better and more confident at speaking your truth.

Ensure your mantra is always – I'm doing this because I want the best for my friend. I'm doing this for me because I deserve friends who treat me well and make me feel good. (How is your friend supposed to know that they have hurt your feelings if they don't know?) This can come back to the values that you worked on earlier in the book. Everyone is different and with that comes beautiful moments and sometimes a few hiccups along the way.

High school takes us out of feeling comfortable and when we are taken away from feeling comfortable it feels the opposite (uncomfortable). This is what makes it hard! This also means that you have the opportunity to start maturing in the way you approach your social life. No longer will your parent or guardian organise your social life – you do! This type of action requires exercising a level of maturity and kindness that may be unfamiliar to you.

Here is an example: If there are four people in your group and three of you organise to go to the beach or shops – how do you think the other girl feels? If you wouldn't want to be the one left out – don't do it to someone else! This is when empathy starts to be applied.

It helps to walk in the other person's shoes. This means asking yourself, if I was her:

1) how would I feel?

2) how would I rock up at school the next day and look the other girls in the eyes?

Asking for help

When you go to high school there are a few different options you have to access if you need any help or guidance:

- 💗 School Counsellor – they are part of the school support and are there to support you

- 💗 Year Advisor – they are the person that is dedicated to looking after the wellbeing for all of Year 7 students

- 💗 Administration office – the people in the general office know everything and everyone at the school – tell them you need to speak to someone and they will coordinate it.

The adults around you have been in the same situation as you, they have spoken to so many new faces – they are there to help you – you are not the first and you won't be the last!

Exploring tricky situations

Friend dynamics

Chloe and Zoe

Chloe and Zoe have been tight friends for a couple of months.

Chloe talks about all of her really good friends when they aren't around – she talks about what they have done to offend her, what they look like (in a negative way), what they have said and makes comments about how she would do things differently when anyone else is trying something new or different...

Chloe has been doing this for so long she doesn't even realise what she is doing – it's now part of how she is every day.

After a while, Zoe thinks to herself – what is she saying about me when I am not around?

Zoe starts to distance herself from Chloe and then there is a drama because Chloe has told everyone that Zoe is ignoring her. Next minute, everyone is asking Zoe why she isn't speaking to Chloe anymore.

Zoe has a couple options:

Option a) she tells everyone why but doesn't tell Chloe directly – Chloe then hears from someone else.

Option b) she speaks to Chloe face to face and tells her that they have fun together but she is worried because Chloe speaks negatively about everyone else all the time and it makes her feel uncomfortable – it's not how she wants a friendship to be.

What could be another option? (You may have a really great option that you want to capture here)

....

....

Which is the easiest option? Why?

....

....

Which is the hardest option? Why?

....

....

It's natural to talk about others – we all approach school and friends differently, but when someone else's life is the only thing you talk about then maybe it's time to find a way of having fun with friends by doing something else. Try going to the beach for a walk, doing an exercise workout on YouTube, playing a game, going to the park, doing some craft or cooking something together.

To be a good friend sometimes means that it's hard work. You need to be honest in a caring and kind way. This can be really uncomfortable but if you value the friendship then honesty will make the relationship grow stronger.

If it turns out that they just aren't your tribe / kind of person, you have a couple of options.

1. Keep your distance – just stay away from people who don't make you feel good about yourself. It's called looking after yourself first.

2. Do not let someone else dictate how you feel. Remind yourself that if someone is being mean, the likelihood is that they aren't very happy with themselves and so they want others to feel bad with them. If it happens

regularly, this is serious, don't ignore it and TELL a teacher or someone you trust. You have your superpower character strengths that can help you through this and you need adult support. Don't take it on yourself – get a helping hand.

3. Remember teachers are there to teach class subjects and they are also there to be your guide in navigating some of this stuff. If a teacher you like and trust can't help, they will find someone else to help you. This is what the high school community is about – preparing and raising kids for the adult world which includes emotional support.

In tricky situations, it's often nothing to do with you. It is important to always think a bit bigger than yourself. This can help to look after yourself and build on your friendships.

Anita and Abby

Anita asked her friend Abby if she wanted to have a sleepover. Abby said she didn't want to as she was tired. On her phone that night Anita saw that Abby was at Charlotte's house having a sleepover.

Anita was hurt and upset.

Option a) Anita sends a message to Abby saying, 'I know where you are and I'm really upset. Why are you there when I invited you over?'

Option b) Anita turns off her phone and decides to speak to Abby the next day, face-to-face. Anita tells Abby how she feels by saying 'I saw you were at Charlotte's last night, I was upset because you said no to me. Have I done something that I don't know about?' Abby explains that she had something going on with her family, Charlotte had known her since kindy and she just wanted to hang out with Charlotte. She said she was sorry and should have told her the truth to begin with but she didn't want to hurt her feelings.

In this example, Abby's choice to hang out with Charlotte is clearly not about Anita. This can be the case in many situations – it's probably not about you. Here's some more examples:

Maddie

Maddie's on her phone when you are talking to her, she isn't paying attention to what you are saying. What you need to remind yourself of is that Maddie has made a choice to be on her phone and not focus on you. What can you control in this situation? You could feel that she is ignoring you or being rude to you but there is a chance it's not about you.

Walk in the other person's shoes – what could be going on for Maddie? Make space for understanding instead of being accusatory or thinking it's a reflection on you. Sometimes it's easy to get upset about these situations when it's actually easier for you and the other person not to take it to heart.

Danya and Tayla

Danya and Tayla are talking, they stop talking the minute you arrive. Your stomach sinks and your instant reaction is to think they were talking about you – gossiping or saying something unkind. Instead, consider the fact that they could be confiding in each other and it has nothing to do with you at all.

If you really do think it's about you, pause, consider, and think about what you want to do about it.

Option a) talk to them / speak up

Option b) walk away and find another group

Are there any other options you would consider? Have a think about what would work for you or what advice you would give a friend.

You can train yourself to think about the other person as opposed to yourself – you need to be kind to yourself and practise empathy.

Strong people don't put others down, they lift them up.
Michael P. Watson (Author)

I don't know anyone – what happens if I don't find anyone that I like?

If you are new to town or do not know anyone at your new high school, remember that you may not be the only one. Kids have come to high school from all sorts of backgrounds and locations. Being new is certainly not a disadvantage. Use it to your advantage and as a talking point when meeting someone for the first time.

I've always found it hard to make friends – is high school going to be the same?

Maybe not! When you get to high school you will be with more kids and this means more variety in options of personalities and people. Try to keep an open mind and you never know who you might meet. Tap into what you know about yourself, your smarts and your character.

I find it hard to tell friends how I feel because I don't want to hurt their feelings – what can I do?

By telling your friends how you feel when a friend says something that hurts your feelings, they can learn more about you. You will know as your friendship progresses whether they learn more about you and adjust their behaviour and words to suit you – that's when you can be more yourself with them, develop trust and your friendship can become stronger.

It can be exhausting thinking about all of the scenarios that may play out – so let's talk about doing this confidently.

We open up to new opportunities when we are prepared to give things a go.

If you are someone who doesn't like to speak up, one really great option you have is to practise speaking up! Believe in yourself – don't overthink it – start speaking up and after a while it will become second nature (like your times tables that you have been practising since Year 1!).

I'm in a group of girls and there are a couple of them who are unkind and bitchy – what can I do?

Ask yourself – what makes their opinion matter? Some people are just unkind or for whatever reason, they don't like you but what would happen if you decided to ignore their opinion? What would be an advantage and what would be a disadvantage?

I know I have been a bit unkind but that seems to be the way people expect me to be now because I was like this at primary school. I want to change but I don't know how...

You are amazingly courageous to ask this question! First step is to start giving compliments instead of unkind remarks. Complete random acts of kindness; acknowledge that you weren't that nice a person in primary school and that you are trying to make changes now. Do one thing each day to build towards who you want to be from now on.

Sometimes I don't know when to stop with what I am saying – we are all having a laugh and then I know I go too far – what could I do to change this?

Check in and ask yourself, if you were to have an adult listening, what would they say or do when you are joking around? If in your heart you know that you have 'gone too far' and the joke has tipped from being fun to being mean or cruel then it's okay to STOP! It's okay to acknowledge that you went too far and apologise.

I don't like saying 'no' to friends when they ask me to hang out – what can I do?

Many of us find it hard to say no, even when we know that it would be kinder to. Sometimes it's better to be honest and say that you feel bad or awkward about saying 'no'. Everyone wants to know where they stand

and it's much better to say it up front to avoid the drama. There is a difference if you start becoming unreliable and don't follow through on what you say you will do on a regular basis.

What if I don't like any of the girls and I want to hang out with the boys – is that okay?

Absolutely – just because most of the time girls hang out with girls and boys hang out with boys, doesn't mean you can't. It's about finding the people in your world that you enjoy being with.

What happens if someone else lets me down and I can't move on from it?

It is important to acknowledge you have been treated badly. Think about how this makes you feel and then move on, letting that feeling go.

Feelings are just visitors, let them come and go.
Mooji, a Spiritual Teacher

What can I do to make myself feel good each day @ school?

- 💗 Think of a couple of healthy thoughts that you could bring into your daily routine.

- 💗 Have mental strength – practise what you are grateful for. This is like a muscle workout for your brain – you get a stronger mind when you think about what you are thankful for. Write them down and don't forget them.

- 💗 Acknowledge that it is okay and normal to feel sad sometimes – it's actually good for us to feel this so we know what different emotions feel like.

- 💗 Don't compare yourself to other people – you are your own person. What could you do to make yourself stronger today than you were yesterday? That's all that should matter.

Amaya – I'm really good at holding a grudge – I am trying not to because I know it's not good for me but I know I do it – it feels like a really hot rock burning in my hand and I can't get rid of it until I start thinking about what I am grateful for – that always helps with the rock's temperature!

What should I do if I think I am being bullied?

You can make sure in the first instance that you talk to a trusted adult. I called on expert Jess from Bullyology to answer this question.

'There are several types of bullying you might find yourself facing and it's important to know the differences:

Physical bullying –

This is the most obvious form of bullying and the easiest to identify – it's when a bigger, stronger or more aggressive person physically attacks a target in some way. Like all forms of bullying, it can sometimes involve multiple aggressors (or targets).

Verbal attacks –

Verbal bullies use words as weapons to gain control or power over their chosen target. They often single out those who seem 'different' in how they look, act or dress. This kind of bullying is more common than physical bullying but harder to pin down, since it often occurs when nobody else is around. In many ways, verbal bullying can be even more dangerous than a physical attack because its effects can leave deep emotional scars and mess up the bullying target's self-esteem.

Cyberbullying −

This is bullying that happens online. It can involve anything from sending hurtful texts, photos or videos to spreading vicious rumours on social media or posting threatening messages. With tech on the rise, it's a growing problem and especially serious because it's harder to escape from than face-to-face bullying. Being a cyberbullying target can feel overwhelming and never-ending. The Internet makes it easier for perpetrators to feel insulated or detached from their cruelty and in some cases, the target may not even know exactly who is bullying them.

Sexual bullying −

Sexual bullying comes in many forms: sexting, uninvited touching, sexual name-calling, propositioning, crude gestures, vulgar comments, exposing the victim to pornographic material, etc. Sexual bullying is harmful, repeated and humiliating to the target. In some cases, it can be a stepping stone to sexual assault.

Bullying based on prejudice −

Some bullies target those they see as different because of their race, religion or sexual orientation. This repeated abuse can expand into other forms of bullying and can often be quite severe, leading to major emotional distress for the target.

Emotional bullying (relational aggression) −

This kind of social manipulation is the 'sneakiest' kind of bullying. The bully spreads rumours, ostracises the target from a particular group, breaks confidences or manipulates situations to hurt the target's social standing and boost their own.'

If you believe you are experiencing any of these you should speak to a trusted adult or any of the suggestions in the 'Asking for help' section.

What should I do if I see someone else being bullied?

Again, I called on Jess to answer this question. She calls people who stand up for others Upstanders.

There is plenty we can all do to become upstanders when we see a bullying situation unfold:

- tell the bully to stop – and explain why what they're doing is wrong

- see if you can get a few of your friends to join forces with other upstanders to present a united front against bullying

- be a friend to the target – ask if they're okay; support them in any way you can by telling your parent or carer if you don't know what to do yourself

- make it clear to others that you won't participate in bullying behaviours of any kind

- never stand by, watch and do nothing (ask yourself: what if it was me?)

- never encourage bullying behaviour – this makes you a co-bully

- never respond to messages, emails or photos that might be upsetting or offensive – this includes 'liking' or sharing a social media post that you know isn't kind

- don't spread hurtful gossip

- your school will have an anti-bullying policy – have a read of it

- focus on the facts: know the 'who, when, where, how and why' and provide an accurate account of everything you saw or experienced in relation to the abuse

- ask an adult for advice.

Everyone is on their phones at lunchtime and recess and I don't feel like there is anyone to chat to – what can I do? (Not applicable in some schools and currently the State of Victoria!)

You could explore a couple of options. You could agree with a friend that you go on your phones for half of lunch and then do something else or find one person that isn't on their phone and take a step towards chatting to them. One way of doing this is by counting down from five in your head and being courageous enough to ask them if they would like to play handball, go for a walk, go to the library or anything else you can think of. Ask yourself, what is the worst thing that can happen – they say no? Yep, that's tough and if you don't ask you will never know. You have two options right now – ask them or watch everyone else on their phones... and if they say 'yes' you may well have made a new friend!

5 4 3 2 1

Getting ready

PRE first day

- If it's an option, see if you can catch up with any of the girls before school starts at some point over the holidays – everyone is spread out all over the place now so it may be tricky but try and see who can catch up.

- If you are going to the same school as some of your friends, arrange to meet them at the school gate so you can walk in together.

On the first day

- If you don't know anyone – walk in and see where all the other kids are standing that look similar to you – a bit lost, not too confident!

- You will soon be put into individual classes so you will know who is in the same class as you pretty quickly.

- Try to be yourself – it ends up being easier in the long run. If you are yourself from the beginning, you don't have to keep up an 'image' in the longer term since your friends will know who you are.

- All you need to do is talk to one person – remember, everyone is in the same situation and everything is new. If you find yourself standing by yourself, you won't be the only one.

Positive practices mean that you can be more creative, nicer and kinder to everyone around you.

One way to set yourself up for success is to set a first goal: Finding the toilet or the classroom where you have roll call.

Next goal: that by the end of the first week you know where to go without following others.

Next goal: Once you have nailed that, aim for not having to look at your timetable after each class to see where you are going.

Some high schools have week A and week B just to confuse you even more. If that's the case you will adjust to the rhythm of this schedule within the first term. By the middle of the year you won't even have to think about it, which will mean that you are CONFIDENT at navigating your way around the place and reading a timetable! Woohoo!

Letters from former Year 6 and 7 girls

These girls and women before you have walked in your shoes. Some have travelled the world, gained more experience and had the chance to look back on what their experience was like in the transition to high school. Others are still there and have recent experience.

Dear Me,

High school is on the horizon. Secretly you are scared and a little angry about changing. What will it be like? You still can't believe you are going to be alone. School without your two best friends. Why can't you be Catholic like them? Sure, you know people going to the community high school, but it's not the same. They will be together. Since that first day in kindergarten, you have always been together. It all seems unfair. Life in primary school this year has been amazing. Trips to the movies and shopping with friends. Parties. It has been an exciting year. You had a lead role in the school musical and your partner for the Year 6 farewell is one of the best-looking guys in school. Life is good. There has been way too much fun.

So it happened. You are here in high school, minus your two best friends. At first, lunch breaks were long and a little lonely.

There are so many more people. Last week, there was even a fight between two boys in the quadrangle, which everyone ran to cheer. You have never seen anything like that before. There are different classes. You even have a class in woodwork, which you will surprise yourself when you come first in the year due to your crafting of a wooden spoon. Your parents will find this hysterically funny. Art, History, Drama and English are your favourites though. It was during English classes that you made new friendships and the loss of your good friends started to ease. It took a little time to let them in, but when you did it opened up a whole heap of new possibilities. Change can be scary if you are not surrounded by the friends who have known you the longest. Just be you.

You never know who you may attract. Like a magnet, you will be drawn to them. Open yourself to what is around you. Even at times when it can be lonely, overwhelming or confronting, there are pockets of kindness and friendship to discover. You will find your tribe.

Love 45-year-old you xx

To my crazy 11-year-old self,

Be patient! High school for most is only six years long. Through-out the first few terms of Year 7 you are going to be getting in the groove for the rest of high school! It gets a lot easier and you get to know the teachers a bit better — especially the ones that look out for you as a person, not just a student!

Don't sweat the small stuff. You will look back at this time and remember it — yes, it's the small things that matter sometimes, but it's not worth getting worked up over.

There is no such thing as a time machine. You will never get this time back so don't wish it away!

Love you.

Dear Me,

I really don't want to be moving – why can't things just stay the same as they have always been? Everything is comfortable, I just want to press pause and keep on having fun with my friends who have known me for ever.

I'm really trying to hide how I feel because I don't want to get upset and spoil the last few months of fun. In bed at night I cry with anticipation and worry, and the next day I try and forget about it.

The last day of term is so much fun, we sign each other's shirts, laugh at and with each other. I can't wait to see the back of a couple of the girls though – they have always been mean and I am really glad that they won't be at the new school.

I try not to think about the new school until the week before. Summer has been so much fun!

On the first day of school, I walk into the large playground a bit worried that I am going to be different or stand out – I just want to be the same as everyone else but they have all their friends and I feel I'm the only one that's new. I go straight to the toilets, looking at each person's face as I walk to see if I see anyone that looks friendly. When I get to the toilets I go into a cubicle, take a deep breath and tell myself it's going to be okay – what's the worst that can happen?

I walk out and there is a girl who looks my age and like me, a bit awkward and she politely smiles – inside, I am cheering cause she looks friendly!

I say to her – 'Hi, is it your first day too?' She smiles and nods. I am SOOO relieved – I ask if she wants to walk together out to the playground. We don't talk too much but having someone with me gives me a boost!

Her name was Yvonne and for the first term we hang out each day, slowly getting to know each other. We aren't in the same class but at lunchtime we hunt each other out.

When I look back, I think it actually made me really strong going to a new school where I knew nobody. At the time, I felt so self-conscious and worried and now I realise that when I go to new places and meet new people it's actually a bit easier every time.

Love

Me xx

To my Year-6-self,

Well, this is it. Soon you'll be starting at a new school, in a new city. You don't know anyone yet, but don't worry – you will soon.

Don't be too sad about leaving your old friends, you're all off on your own adventures. Be happy for them, and they'll be happy for you, too. I want to warn you though, the next few years will be hard. The people you become friends with in Year 7 won't be the people you're friends with in Year 12. But don't worry – the friends you leave school with will stick with you for a long time (they're even coming to your 20th birthday in a few weeks!).

School is annoying, and it can be really hard sometimes, but your education is important – value it, and work at it. Not everyone gets the chance to go to school, so do not waste this opportunity.

High school is a lot of fun, it's also really tiring. That's okay though. That's how you know it's something worth going through. It's how you learn who you are. In your time at school, you're going to win netball championships, be in plays, get a job, go to parties, learn to drive, make amazing friends and by the time you walk out the school gates for the last time, you won't believe how much you've accomplished in six years.

Over the next little while, you're going to grow up – a lot – and so is everyone around you. You won't all be on the same timeline. You'll find that you grow up a lot faster than your other friends, and a lot slower than others. They might be ready for things before you are, and you might feel a little left behind. That's why you make friends with different people, and why you don't always get along with everyone. Maturity is funny like that. Just focus on you, on when you are ready. If it doesn't feel right, it probably isn't. And when it doesn't feel right – tell someone (your parents, a teacher, a coach, your uncle or aunty etc.).

Now, the first few weeks of Year 7 are a little scary, but don't let it put you off. You'll miss the bus a few times and will shed a few tears along the way. You get the hang of it in the end, and you're the most independent of all your friends. There are going to be some hiccups along the way – you'll fail an exam or two, and it's okay to be disappointed when things don't go your way. Let yourself be sad sometimes.

Whenever you're feeling down, let yourself cry. Let yourself be so mad that you think you might explode. Then, stand up, go outside, make yourself a cup of tea and have a shower. The only person who can pull you out of the dark is you. You're more powerful than you know.

The point is, high school is really hard – growing up, meeting new people, learning so many new things – but it's so worth it. By the time you're finishing your HSC and moving out of home, you won't believe how much you've done and how much you've changed. Make the most of it all, you'll miss seeing your friends every day, and sitting in the sun at lunch. Treasure this time while you have it.

So, as a quicky summary, here is a list of things to remember:

1. The people who are meant to be in your life will be there – let the rest continue their own journey.

2. STUDY! You're in school to learn – don't waste this time.

3. Grow up at your own speed, not everyone else's.

4. Let yourself feel – the happy, the sad, all of it.

5. You're pretty freakin' cool. No one can take that from you.

Lots of love, 19-year-old you

To my 11-year-old self,

Don't be overwhelmed by the unfamiliarity of your new class, you are one of the lucky ones who has the same friends as you did in primary school. Try your best and embrace the new challenges and know that the more you put in the more satisfying and rewarding it will be.

Love me xxx

Dear me,

You have always been told to work hard and that you have to try your best – why are you so worried about not meeting people's expectations?

You love sport and hate academics. If you had done your homework, you wouldn't have got into so much trouble!

You always trusted people and you helped bring out the confidence in others. This will be the same for the rest of your life as you always manage to get the best out of others by finding their strengths and focusing on the positive.

Being kind and gentle to your friends and having fun helped you through moving into high school. You were always a good listener and people told you their problems because they trusted you. Just remember to look after yourself and not take on all of their problems – you can't solve everything!

Love your 74-year-old self

Hello lovely one,

You're about to start high school so I'm going to help you do better than I did.

Here it is in a nutshell:

1. Work out who you are. Your future friends can't find you if they don't recognise you.

2. Do the right thing for you first. You don't have to look after everyone else's feelings before your own.

3. Power plays are stupid and don't help anyone. If someone tries it on, ask if they're okay before responding with your dapper wit. The last word doesn't matter if someone gets hurt.

4. Listen to your instincts. Yep, that's your tummy. If tummy is unhappy – stop! Take a moment. Really see what's going on.

5. Be your own best friend.

It took me too long to work all this out. The only person I need to be is me, and I'm wonderful. I don't have to model my behaviour on other people (or fictional characters – though that really is fun!) to fit in. I just have to be me to find my tribe, my people, my friends.

I hope you learn to love you much sooner than I did.

You're worth it and so much more, you beautiful dreamer.

HUGE HUGS. Squeeeeeze! I know you can feel it.

I love you.

44-year-old me

I know – I'm so old, right? It's super weird. Oh – that's a great point number 6!

6. You never feel like a grown-up – you just keep learning and trying to be your best self as you get older (and older). So love the journey and remember there is learning in every experience, good or bad or boring. Love you!

Dear year six me...

Going to a new school with a new class where you know barely anyone from your primary school might sound daunting, but it was one of the best things. I have made so many new friends and have a completely different friend group. I am still navigating my way through high school but know that each opportunity presented to you usually has an exciting outcome so why not have a go!

I have been told that I haven't changed since year six and that frustrates me. The things I have been through in the past two years have tested me and helped me grow as a person. I have gone through dark times but still managed to come out with a smile on my face. One thing that I have learnt through this time is that just because someone isn't crying doesn't mean they're not on the inside. The majority of teens are struggling but choose to put up a wall and keep going, because we're afraid, because no one else is admitting it. Why should we put ourselves out there and be rejected again?

I'm sorry, sorry that no one told you that as soon as that bubble of primary school bliss is popped, your safety net disappears with it. High school – nothing like what I had imagined. In primary school they told you it was going to be okay, physical activity is important and to do your best. They should have told us what drugs are, it's okay to have emotions, what high school would actually be like. Until I reached year 7, I had never heard the word vape, but now all I seem to see is another person being suspended because of them. Year six is your last chance to be a child so use it, before they expect you to act like an adult, be mature, responsible, happy, independent and obedient. Because that is hard to manage on top of social life, home life and what's considered the most important – grades.

Overall, if I were to go back, I would tell my younger self to appreciate everything and to try hard but not set the expectations of myself so high. It's okay not to be the best.

xoxo,

14-year-old you

To my dear Year 6 self,

If only I was able to have received this letter myself when I was your age. Oh, the difference this may have made to the way I might have approached a number of things that you are yet to experience. I know at your age you think an adult doesn't understand what you are feeling and going through and therefore couldn't possibly offer you advice on how to overcome some obstacles. But as the adult you, I have to say you are wrong! You should listen more to those around you and those offering you guidance and coaching. One day when you are my age, you will be thankful that people with experience and wisdom took the time to coach you. You will be where you are because of those exceptional people... and that's a good thing!

I want you to know that it is okay that you aren't the same as the people all around you. Being the only female in Years 5 & 6 in a small country school hasn't been easy for you. You have had your fair share of pokes and prods over time that have made you put up an armour to protect you from the next round of bullets. What you must realise is that armour you have put up to protect you from the bullets coming in is also protecting you from showing your authentic self and letting that beam of sunshine come out. When you do show that beam, you will see that people respect and value who you are, and being different (and proud of that) is what will make you so successful in the life that you have ahead of you.

It will take you by surprise in Year 7 when you get there and realise that now you do have some like-minded people around you, that you are more confident to show your true self, put that armour down and that is when you do start to shine. When you start to shine, you get confidence and continue to show the value you can add in many different aspects of life. That lesson should just be adopted through the rest of your life regardless of when you find yourself back in the minority again and feeling like an armour needs to be put up. Because you will come across that time in your life again, but what you need to do is not put the armour up and just continue to be proud of the difference you bring to a situation and how inclusive people will embrace that.

What I am doing for you...well...what the adult you is doing for the new and upcoming Year 6 students of today...is working very hard to make sure that people of my era respect and understand the importance of being inclusive so that diversity is respected and people can bring their authentic self to a situation and do that proudly. We have a way to go yet, but I promise you that we are committed to that cause and we are starting to see some movement.

Take care of yourself...and one last final bit of advice...don't ever think you can't...because you can!

From the adult you, who is so proud of what you do over the next 32 years ☺

My term one journal

1ST WEEK CHECK IN

At the beginning of the week, I felt:

Now I feel (it's okay if it's the same – it's only the first week!):

I think I need some help with (we all need a helping hand no matter how old we are, so write a few things down):

I am grateful for (who / what):

I learned about (can be academic / life):

I want to know more about (can be academic / life):

One thing I am going to do differently next week to make it easier than my first week:

2ND WEEK CHECK IN

At the beginning of the week, I felt:

Now I feel (it's okay if it's the same as the previous week):

I think I need some help with (we all need a helping hand no matter how old we are, so write a few things down):

I am grateful for (who / what):

I learned about (can be academic / life):

I want to know more about (can be academic / life):

One thing I am going to do differently next week to make it easier than my second week:

3RD WEEK CHECK IN

At the beginning of the week, I felt:

Now I feel (it's okay if it's the same as the previous week):

I think I need some help with (we all need a helping hand no matter how old we are, so write a few things down):

I am grateful for (who / what):

I learned about (can be academic / life):

I want to know more about (can be academic / life):

One thing I am going to do differently next week to make it easier than my third week:

4TH WEEK CHECK IN

At the beginning of the week, I felt:

Now I feel (it's okay if it's the same as the previous week):

I think I need some help with (we all need a helping hand no matter how old we are, so write a few things down):

I am grateful for (who / what):

I learned about (can be academic / life):

I want to know more about (can be academic / life):

One thing I am going to do differently next week to make it easier than my fourth week:

5ᵀᴴ WEEK CHECK IN

At the beginning of the week, I felt:

Now I feel (it's okay if it's the same as the previous week):

I think I need some help with (we all need a helping hand no matter how old we are, so write a few things down):

I am grateful for (who / what):

I learned about (can be academic / life):

I want to know more about (can be academic / life):

One thing I am going to do differently next week to make it easier than my fifth week:

6TH WEEK CHECK IN

At the beginning of the week, I felt:

Now I feel (it's okay if it's the same as the previous week):

I think I need some help with (we all need a helping hand no matter how old we are, so write a few things down):

I am grateful for (who / what):

I learned about (can be academic / life):

I want to know more about (can be academic / life):

One thing I am going to do differently next week to make it easier than my sixth week:

7TH WEEK CHECK IN

At the beginning of the week, I felt:

Now I feel (it's okay if it's the same as the previous week):

I think I need some help with (we all need a helping hand no matter how old we are, so write a few things down):

I am grateful for (who / what):

I learned about (can be academic / life):

I want to know more about (can be academic / life):

One thing I am going to do differently next week to make it easier than my seventh week:

8TH WEEK CHECK IN

At the beginning of the week, I felt:

Now I feel (it's okay if it's the same as the previous week):

I think I need some help with (we all need a helping hand no matter how old we are, so write a few things down):

I am grateful for (who / what):

I learned about (can be academic / life):

I want to know more about (can be academic / life):

One thing I am going to do differently next week to make it easier than my eighth week:

9TH WEEK CHECK IN

At the beginning of the week, I felt:

Now I feel (it's okay if it's the same as the previous week):

I think I need some help with (we all need a helping hand no matter how old we are, so write a few things down):

I am grateful for (who / what):

I learned about (can be academic / life):

I want to know more about (can be academic / life):

One thing I am going to do differently next week to make it easier than my ninth week:

10TH WEEK CHECK IN

At the beginning of the week, I felt:

Now I feel (it's okay if it's the same as the previous week):

I think I need some help with (we all need a helping hand no matter how old we are, so write a few things down):

I am grateful for (who / what):

I learned about (can be academic / life):

I want to know more about (can be academic / life):

One thing I am going to do differently next term to make it easier than my tenth week:

Other helping hands

As part of developing this book I did research to see what support is available should you like to access it. I trust they will give you a helping hand.

A few websites:

Institute on Character
The FREE character strengths assessment talked about on page 7 is available at https://www.viacharacter.org/survey/account/register# youth. You will need adult permission and an email address to complete it.

kidshelpline
This website is great for reading stories, getting help and referring to additional resources for anything that might be bothering you just now. https://kidshelpline.com.au/kids

Beyond Blue
If you are going through a tough time, this is another website that you can get resources from and get access to speak, text or just connect with an online community. https://www.beyondblue.org.au/who-does-it-affect/young-people

Pick&Mix
Lunchbox handy hints from http://heas.health.vic.gov.au/. There is a really easy-to-use poster outlining some great options about what to consider for your lunch and what you need to make a great variety of nutrients for your growing body.

Bullyology

Jess from Bullyology responded to a couple of questions in the 'Problem Solving' section. You can access her website and further information here. https://bullyology.com/be-an-upstander-in-education/

Headspace

The Headspace App is free for kid meditations that last for up to nine minutes. There are paid subscription options but you don't have to buy them. This app helps with meditation and mindfulness (which basically means helping you to be aware of how you are feeling), some breathing exercises and stories to relax you and create calmness. https://www.headspace.com

Smiling Mind

The Smiling Mind app helps you to build awareness of what's happening with your mind and body. This app will help you focus, be calm and kind to yourself and others. https://www.smilingmind.com.au/

Happyfeed

The Happyfeed – Gratitude Journal & Daily Mood Diary is an easy way to track three things that you are grateful for each day. https://www.happyfeed.co

Recommended Reads

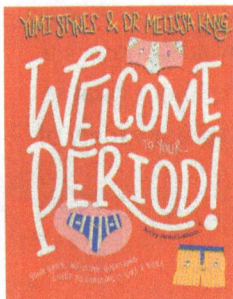

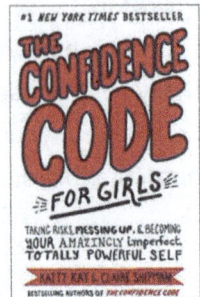

'I'm going to do what I want to do.
I'm going to be who I really am.
I'm going to figure out what that is.'
Emma Watson

Thank Yous!

This book would never have happened if it hadn't been for my daughter Libby starting high school in 2020. Libby, you inspired and guided me to do this. Your enthusiasm, advice on themes, colour palettes and illustrations are what have made this the beautiful book that it is. Thanks for being my partner on this project and of course my daughter!

To all the girls and women who were open, courageous and trusting in sharing their experiences. Your stories and advice will give optimism and strength to any girl entering into this stage of their education and life.

Feedback or discussions along the way on the numerous drafts or ideas for content: Daniel, Elspeth, Emma, Isobell, Jane, Karen, Kate, Kathleen, Kirsten, Lorraine, Melanie, Natalie and Natarsha, I so very much appreciate your interest, time and energy in contributing to making this a resource that is intended to enable girls to have a confident start to high school!

To Olly and my mum Tish for always giving unwavering support in anything that I try!

Printed in November 2021
by Rotomail Italia S.p.A., Vignate (MI) - Italy